little
scribe

Pick a Picture, **Write a REPORT!**

by Kristen McCurry

CAPSTONE PRESS
a capstone imprint

A+ Books are published by Capstone Press,
1710 Roe Crest Drive, North Mankato, Minnesota 56003
www.capstonepub.com

For all the teachers in Marshalltown, Iowa. —KM

Library of Congress Cataloging-in-Publication Data
McCurry, Kristen.
  Pick a picture, write a report! / by Kristen McCurry.
    pages cm. — (A+Books: Little Scribe)
  Summary: "Introduces report writing to children using photographs as idea prompts"— Provided by
publisher.
  Audience: Ages 5-8
  ISBN 978-1-4765-4239-3 (library binding)
  ISBN 978-1-4765-5106-7 (paperback)
  ISBN 978-1-4765-5951-3 (eBook PDF)
1. Report writing—Juvenile literature. 2. Photographs—Juvenile literature. I. Title.
LB1047.3.M39 2014
808.02—dc23   2013032323

Thanks to our adviser for her expertise, research, and advice:
Kelly Boswell, reading consultant and literacy specialist

Editorial Credits
Kristen Mohn, editor; Heidi Thompson, designer; Charmaine Whitman, production specialist

Photo Credits
Capstone Studio: Karon Dubke, 1, 14, 15 (all); iStockphotos: claudio.arnese, 8-9; NASA, 24-25; National
Geographic Stock: Brian J. Skerry, 21; Science Source: Peter Skinner, 18; Shutterstock: Alexandra Lande, 30,
Andrew F. Kazmierski, 11, Angel Simon, 29 (potter), Anthony Correia, 27, Brad Thompson, 23, Brandon Alms,
cover, 5, Dudarev Mikhail, 13, evantravels, 29 (statue), Mircea BEZERGHEANU, 12, prajit48, 28, Rob Marmion,
17, Vishnevskiy Vasily, 6

Note to Parents, Teachers, and Librarians
This Little Scribe book uses full color photographs and a nonfiction format to introduce the concept of writing
reports. *Pick a Picture, Write a Report!* is designed to be read aloud to a pre-reader or to be read independently
by an early reader. Photographs help listeners and early readers understand the text and concepts discussed.
The book encourages further learning by including the following sections: Table of Contents, Glossary, Read
More, Critical Thinking Using the Common Core, and Internet Sites. Early readers may need assistance using
these features.

Printed in the United States of America in Stevens Point, Wisconsin.
092013   007773WZS14

Table of Contents

What Is a Report?

A report is writing that explains or describes something. It provides facts and details about a topic. A report can be short or long. You can write a report about anything that interests you, such as animals, history, sports, or nature.

Here is a report on chameleons.

Chameleons are reptiles. They are a kind of lizard. Chameleons can change color. They hide by blending in with plants. These lizards live in rain forests in many parts of the world.

Your report might be a mix of words and pictures. You can also tell your report to someone who can help you write it down.

Are you ready to try writing some reports?

Bird Facts

Pictures can help you think of a topic for your report. You can also get information from pictures. What facts can you learn from this photo of a bird's nest? You can use facts from a photo in a report.

6

Make a List

Before you write, make a list of questions you want to answer in your report. This list can help you decide in what order to write your information. It can also help you remember everything you want to write about. A list for your report on a bird's nest might look like this:

- What do baby birds do when they're hungry?

- What do mother birds feed their babies?

- What are the nests made of?

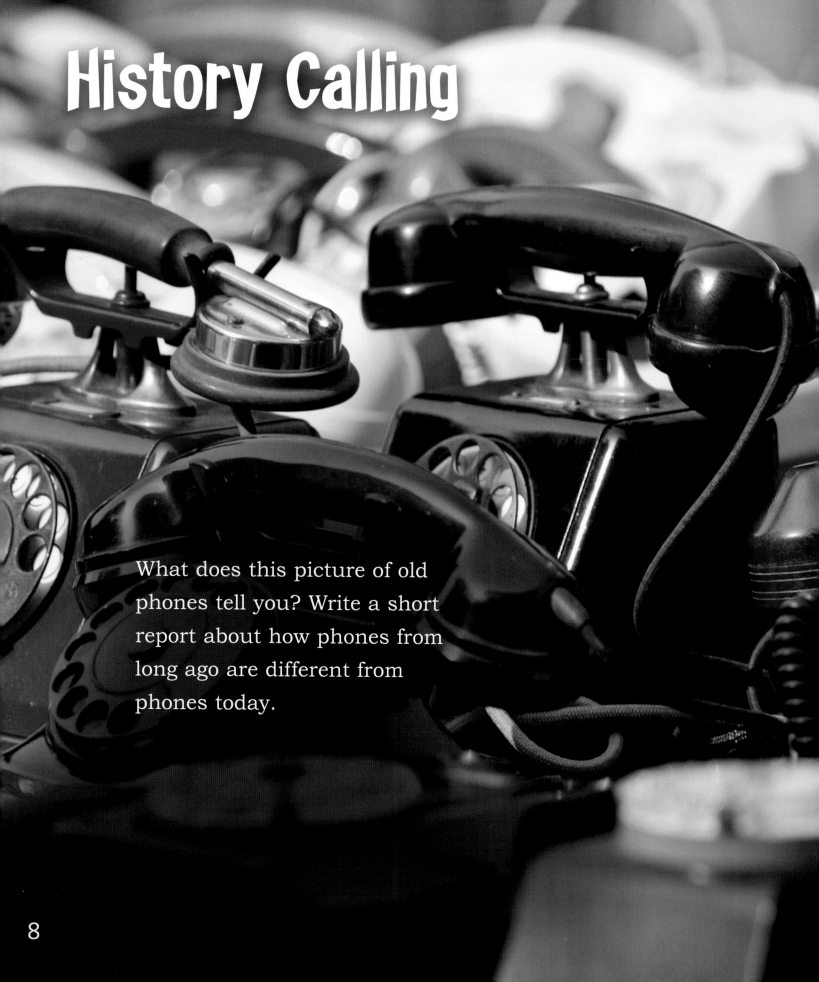

History Calling

What does this picture of old phones tell you? Write a short report about how phones from long ago are different from phones today.

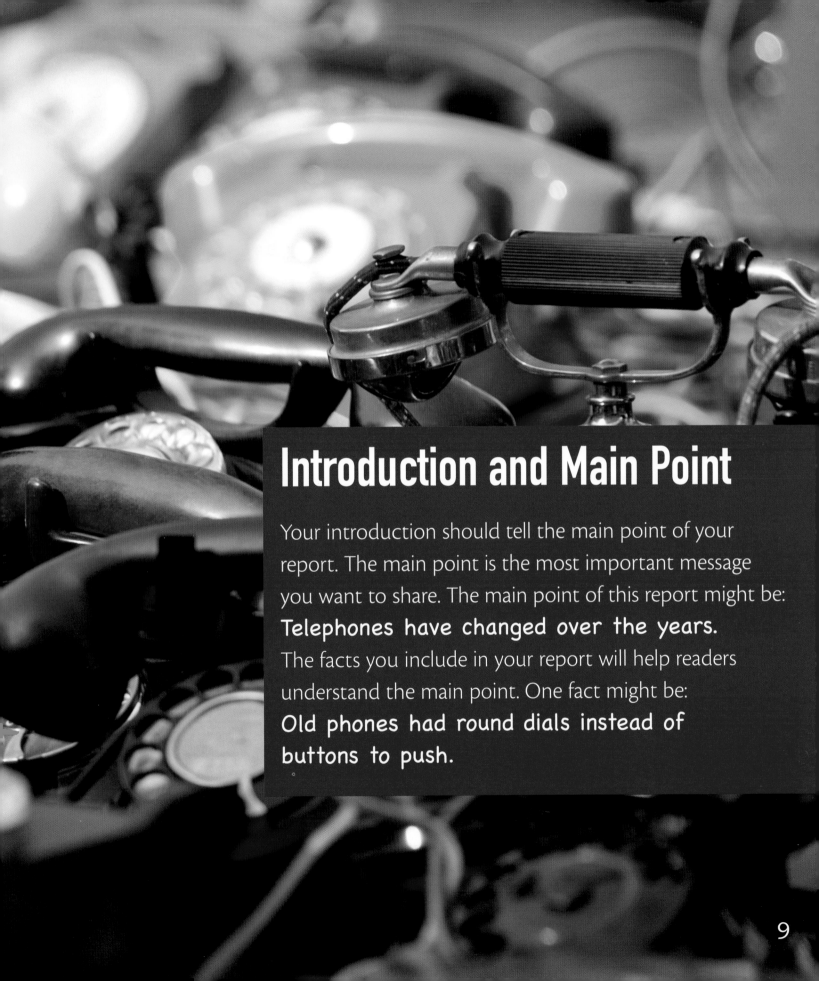

Introduction and Main Point

Your introduction should tell the main point of your report. The main point is the most important message you want to share. The main point of this report might be: **Telephones have changed over the years.**

The facts you include in your report will help readers understand the main point. One fact might be: **Old phones had round dials instead of buttons to push.**

New York City Details

A report might give details about a person, place, or thing. A detail is a small part of something. This photo is of Times Square in New York City. If you were writing a report about New York City, what details could you learn from this photo? Look carefully at the photo for clues.

The Five Senses

Include details about sight, sound, touch, feel, and taste in your report. What sounds do you think you would hear if you were there? What would it feel like to be around so many people?

OBSERVATION

An observation is something you notice. A detail you might observe in this photo is that the people are wearing warm clothing. What does this tell you about the weather?

Comparing Animals

What are the animals in these photos eating? Do all animals eat the same food? Write a report about the kinds of food different animals eat.

Conclusion

A conclusion is a way to end your report. It tells readers what you want them to remember. Your conclusion to this report might be: **Different kinds of animals eat different kinds of food.**

Jack-o'-Lantern Sequence

Some reports describe or explain an order of events. Look at the pictures. Can you write a report about how a jack-o'-lantern is made? Include what would happen before and after these photos. Where do pumpkins come from? What do you do with a jack-o'-lantern after you carve it?

Temporal Words

Temporal words tell when things happen. Use temporal words in your report. Some examples are:

- then
- next
- after
- before
- while
- later
- finally

Giving Directions

Do you know how to do something that you'd like to teach others about? Wash a dog? Grow a plant? Write a report that gives directions about how to do something. Be sure to use temporal words such as "then" and "next" in your report.

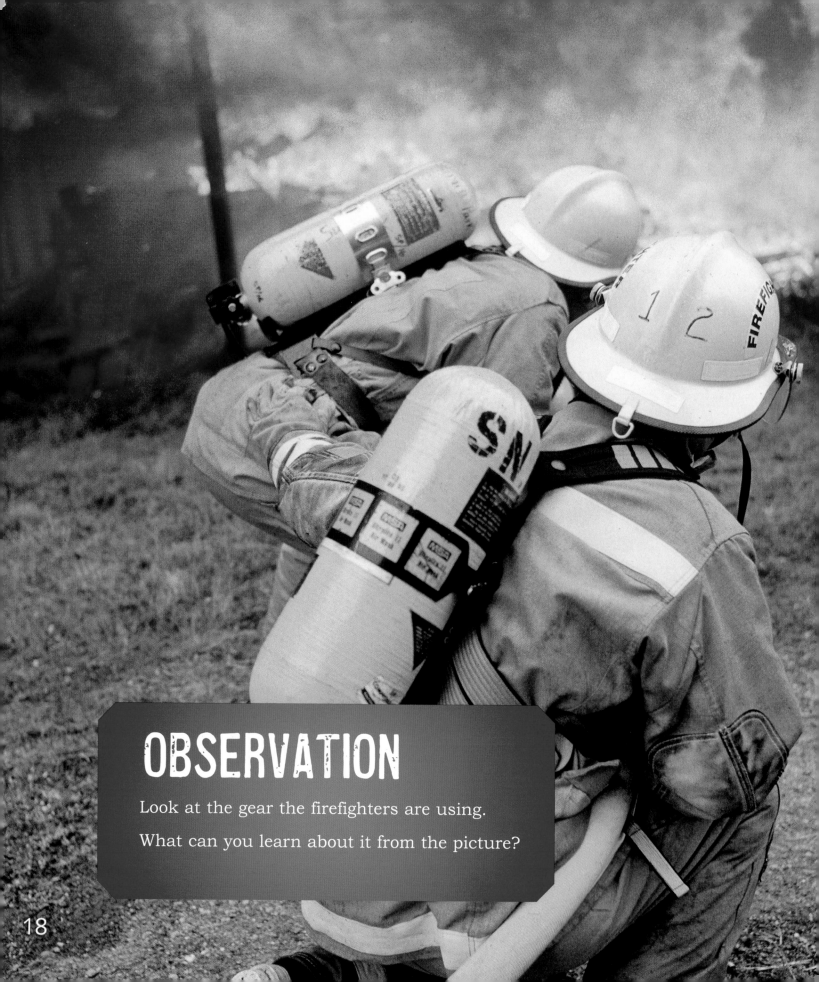

OBSERVATION

Look at the gear the firefighters are using.

What can you learn about it from the picture?

Describing Action

Reports about extreme sports or dangerous jobs can be exciting. You can write about the action. What is happening in this picture? What details about firefighting would you include in a report?

VERBS TELL ACTION

Verbs are action words. Use exciting verbs in your report to help your readers see what's happening. Some verbs in a report about firefighters might be:

- race
- blast
- gasp
- crouch
- aim
- rescue

Community Problems

A report can be about a problem in your community or in the world. This is a way to provide information to others about something that you think is important. You could write a report about littering or pollution. Don't forget your introduction and conclusion.

Science Report

Look around you. Nature is all about science, and science topics are great for reports. Animals, plants, rocks, and the sun are all science topics. What about water? People, plants, and animals all need water. Write a science report about water and why it's important.

GETTING MORE INFORMATION

Sometimes you need more information. For this report you might look for a science book or website about water. Ask your teacher or librarian for help.

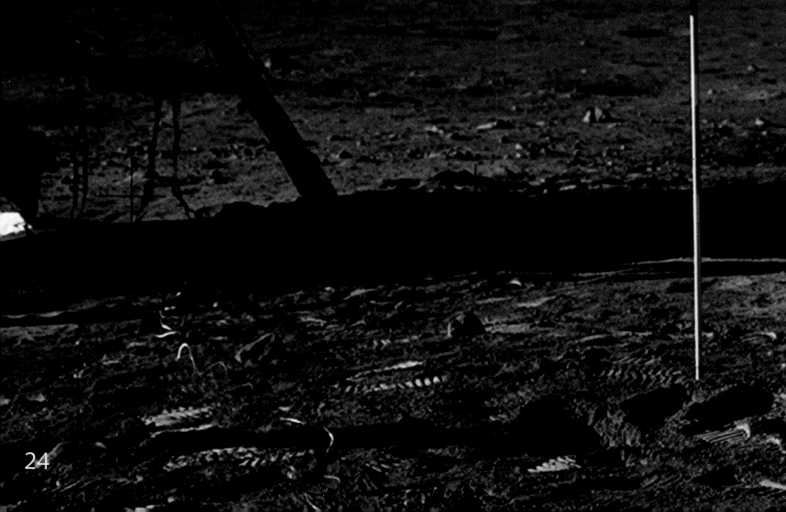

World Events

In 1969 humans first walked on the moon. This photo shows astronaut Buzz Aldrin. Write a report about traveling to space. What does this photo tell you about what it's like on the moon?

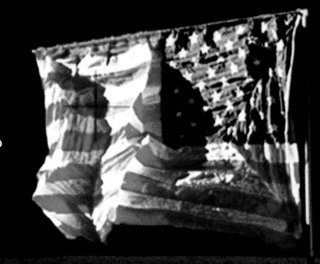

SETTING

The setting is the area where something takes place. What is the setting in this photo? Describe the setting in your report.

Veterans Are Heroes

A military veteran is someone who has served in the armed forces. This veteran is giving a salute.

Why are veterans important? Write a report about them.

BIOGRAPHIES

A biography is a report that tells about a person's life. It might be a famous person. Or it might be a relative or a neighbor you admire. Biographies give facts and help readers learn about someone important.

OBSERVATION

Notice the medals on the veteran's uniform. What do medals mean?

Finding Photos

Browse through a book, magazine, or newspaper to find a photograph that interests you. Write a short report about what the photo shows. If you want to learn more about the topic, ask your teacher or librarian to help you find information

Good job!

You're on your way to becoming a great report writer. Photos are a fun and easy way to get started. But you can write about anything! Just keep your main point in mind and include important facts. Use books and websites to learn more about your topic.

Reports help you share information with others.

Glossary

admire—to like and respect someone

biography—the life story of someone

blend—to fit in with the surroundings

detail—a piece of information; a small part of a bigger thing

event—a thing that happens

litter—to throw garbage on the ground

medal—a piece of metal shaped like a coin that is given for good work done

observe—to watch someone or something closely in order to learn something

pollution—materials that hurt Earth's water, air, and land

salute—a movement with the right hand to give a sign of respect

sequence—a series of things that follow each other in a certain order

setting—the time and place of an event or story

temporal—relating to time

topic—the subject of a piece of writing, talk, speech, or lesson

Read More

Fields, Jan. *You Can Write Excellent Reports*. You Can Write. Mankato, Minn.: Capstone Press, 2012.

Manushkin, Fran. *Stick to the Facts, Katie: Writing a Research Paper with Katie Woo*. Katie Woo, Star Writer. North Mankato, Minn.: Picture Window Books, 2014.

Minden, Cecilia, and Kate Roth. *How to Write a Book Report*. Language Arts Explorer Junior. Ann Arbor, Mich.: Cherry Lake Pub., 2011.

Critical Thinking Using the Common Core

- Read the report on chameleons on page 4. What does the word "blend" mean? What clues in the text help you figure out the meaning? (Craft and Structure)

- On page 7 the author suggests making a list before you write. What are two ways a list can help with your report? What else might you do before you write a report? (Key Ideas and Details)

- Study the list of temporal words on page 15. Explain what temporal words are and how they can help your writing. (Integration of Knowledge and Ideas)

Internet Sites

FactHound offers a safe, fun way to find Internet sites related to this book. All of the sites on FactHound have been researched by our staff.

Here's all you do:

Visit *www.facthound.com*

Type in this code: 9781476542393